Black Girl, You Can Do This

A Book of Love and Empowerment for the Next Generation

Brittni Kirkpatrick

TABLE OF CONTENTS

ACKNOWLEDGMENTS

I am so grateful to have written my first book (of many) and to be in a position of love and influence. It feels incredible. And, I'd like to thank everyone who contributed to my encouragement, motivation, and growth.

Love and gratitude to my best friend, Cristen. My fellow Moonchild and entrepreneur. We have been on this road of growth and power together for ten years. You are beautiful, courageous, and inspiring. You have been there for every high and every low, and I am honored to have someone like you in my life.

Love and light to my fellow author, Michelle. Thank you, thank you, thank you for understanding the power of our synchronistic paths. You are so talented, gifted, creative, and kind. Anytime I needed help focusing on the vision, you were there. Your heart is pure, and I am so ready to see the way you live the life you have created for yourself.

Unconditional love to Stetson for always cultivating the space for me to be exactly who I am. I have never had to be anyone but me, and you have always accepted and encouraged my free-spirited need to explore this world and be original. You understand me, and I am grateful for the life lessons learned. You understand the purpose and the shift. Thank you for listening to all of my weird ideas and words. And may your daughters grow into beautiful, powerful, and authentic women. May they change the world.

Thank you to my dearest friend, Jared. You are the definition of friendship, selflessness, and love. You have helped me to see the world and achieve so many of my goals. You have believed in me from day one and were always there to check me and keep me on my path. May your daughter be proud of the father she has, and may she grow to be everything she wants to be in her precious life.

To all the creatives on this journey with me – I know sometimes, one day is great and the other can be challenging, but we all have the ability to see these things come into fruition. I have had the privilege of knowing some incredibly dope photographers, videographers, musicians, writers, healers, and authentic souls in the last three years. I see you. You're doing what you are passionate about. And I love it. Keep going. Don't quit. Don't stop. Don't let up. We need what you have.

Finally, thank you to Michael Tatonetti. You were sent from God. This book has been on my heart for years, and you helped me see the vision through from start to finish. You are going where you are lead, and you will change so many lives. Thank you, thank you, thank you. May your beautiful daughters be the change we wish to see in the world.

To God, I am grateful. To God, be all the glory and praise. I am humbled, honored, and in awe of the plan you had for me. I will continue to listen to my inner-wisdom as I grow into the woman you have created me to be.

PREFACE

When I started writing this, it never occurred to me that this book would bring me as much healing, clarity, and new life as I intended for it to bring you. The lessons in this book were learned the hard way in most cases. Always having been a stubborn individual, I had to learn things on my own. Always drawn to the offbeat and unconventional, I had no desire to conform. This didn't always work in my favor growing up in a household with parents who followed the paths expected of them. I believe my desire to be hard-headed came from the need to find the true meaning of my life and the truth within myself. It was always of the utmost importance for me to follow the path that was for me and me alone. I needed to be true to myself, to be original, and to be an individual in everything that I did. I wanted to engage in projects and causes that spoke to my soul. I wanted to love, I wanted to do and see, and I wanted to explore the world.

The love letters and lessons in this book are meant to teach you the lessons I wish I had learned, the ones I learned but didn't take heed, and the ones I learned the hard way but hope to keep you from repeating. This book is my effort to bring you love, healing, encouragement, and empowerment. These lessons have made me the woman I am today, and I hope that they will help mold you into the woman you are becoming and choose to be.

Around the time I was finishing writing this book, I heard a man say he felt bad for the next generation because they "don't do anything but get on Snapchat and Instagram." He also stated, "They don't read, they don't think, and they know nothing." It made me cringe, because I thought of all of you and the great potential you hold to change your own lives and the world around you. While it may seem that way to others like him, I couldn't subscribe to what he was saying because I know there is power in your generation. I believe that if you'd only shift your energy and focus on that greatness, you'd be able to move and shake the foundation of your people and your communities. You are more than songs glorifying drug abuse, surgically-enhanced plastic bodies, Snapchat filters, and early sexual activity. You are world-changers, world-travelers, doers, seers, movers, and shakers. You are our future. You were created for a purpose and a reason. And if you have this book, it is not by coincidence or chance.

What I want for you is to skip the dead space of confusion in your teens and early adulthood. It can be a confusing and trying time, especially in today's society. You are faced with social media telling you who you should be, how you should look, and how you should act. You have a world of information and technology at your fingertips, and you can either choose to use it to your advantage or fall victim to the ploy. I wrote this to you as I would have written it to myself. I chose to be for you who I needed when I was your age. I want you to use this book as a personal diary as you begin a journey within yourself, capturing your notes, and completing the reflections at the end of each chapter. My intention is for you to blossom and transform with the flip of each page, using this book as a guide for the evolution of who you are from start to finish.

I have always been concerned with personal growth, and as I wrote this book and poured out my heart, it all came full circle for me. It is so important to me to support other people and to see the potential in each person I meet. I believe that the possibilities are paramount. In order for you to believe the same, you must begin to truly know, understand, and embrace yourself. As you do, you open yourself to the flow and possibilities of this magical life. All I ever wanted was to heal, lead, teach, and write. And I knew I had to shift my focus, step into my power, and create the life that I wanted. I had received too many opportunities and signs of confirmation to write this for you all. And I knew I wanted to live the life God created me to. I prayed and asked God to help cultivate a life that allowed me to thrive in my element. And that is what I want to do for you – to support you, empower you, and cultivate the space for you to thrive as well.

I believe each of you must find your own path and be an individual in all that you do. Life won't always be easy, but the joy, abundance, and greatness of God's creation is worth every moment. As I learned what I needed to about my emotions, my life, and my identity, I was being equipped to share these lessons with you to keep you from heartache, confusion, and the wrong things in life. I had to be everything you needed me to be. I needed to spark the ingenuity, power, creativity, and purpose inside of you.

These words come from the heart, as I've been where most of you are mentally, emotionally, physically, and spiritually. When I think of you, I think of a younger me – young, creative, smart, and trying to grasp an understanding of life. But luckily for you, you don't have to wait until you're my age to figure it out. You don't have to rush to grow up, either. When we take the time to build strong, kind, aware, and powerful youth, then we have a better chance of seeing an equipped and capable next generation thrive instead of more confused adults who need direction and healing from their pasts. You can choose how to move and flow with your life, now.

I am here to assist and inspire you in your natural abilities, gifts, and skills. I am here to encourage you to listen to your inner-wisdom and to be guided by what you know is right. I am here to help you live the lives you've been created to live as your best selves and to your fullest potential. In this book, I contribute my philosophies and unique perspective as a light and example for you.

Throughout this book, we are going to be open and honest about where we currently are in our lives, begin to chip away at what needs to be changed, and begin to create new beliefs on our paths to purpose and truth. We will be using this time and the space to open our hearts and pour them onto the pages. Who we are at the end of this book should be a more evolved version of ourselves than we began – more in love with ourselves, more aware of ourselves, and with more freedom to be our highest, most authentic selves.

This book is written from my heart and soul to teach and guide you in love, empowerment, and truth. You are the next generation of world-changing leaders. Let us begin that journey now; I am ready to hear about the amazing way you transform your life.

CHAPTER ONE
Knowledge of Self

My Dearest Love,

I write this to you from the deepest parts of my heart and soul, and I pray you feel my most unconditional love in every word. There is such a Divine calling on your life, and you were uniquely and divinely created for such a time as this. You are Divine, because your Creator is Divine. You were made in God's image in the unconditional love and perfection of His wisdom.

When I was your age, girl, let me tell you: I was a mess. I had no idea who or what I was or what I was called to do in life. I mean, I knew I was a girl. I knew I was in high school. I knew I loved writing and had been writing since I was 6 years old. I loved music and the theater, but knowledge of self was the furthest thing from my mind. I wasn't thinking about it, and no one was talking about things like that. I had no idea I could be aware of who I was and walk in a purpose or calling. You get up, you go to school, and you do what you're supposed to as a child, a teenager, a daughter, and a student. It wasn't until I was 26 years old that I really began to grasp the concept.

Knowledge of the world around you starts with your knowledge and understanding of self. Once you have knowledge of self and God, you can move about in your daily life unmoved and unshaken by the actions and opinions of others. Darling, if you do not know who you are, this world will most definitely tell you and define you. You are not easily distracted when you have knowledge of self, and you are standing firm on solid foundation. When challenges arise, as they will throughout your life, you are better equipped to handle them without freaking out or losing sight of who you are. It clears the fog of confusion and enables you to walk in the power of who you are.

When you know who you are, you will be able to look within and hear the guidance, answers, comfort, understanding, and love that God has given you from the beginning. Your intuition will guide you. Your intuition is like a compass – that gut feeling about things, people, and situations that are or are not right for you. Never doubt the voice inside of you. We all have a 'knowing' inside of us. When you listen to and trust that wisdom, you are putting faith into the very wisdom, love, and guidance that created you. Your intuition is a gift. Trust in it. The Holy Spirit will always guide you when you ask.

When you appreciate your life and understand your divinity, you will hold yourself to a standard. It is not up to your mom, your dad, your favorite aunt, your friends, the media, and especially not up to a man to love you wholly. You must have that love for yourself first and foremost. If you look for others to make you feel whole, you will never be satisfied. No matter the relationship with your parents (good or unfavorable), the school you go to, the neighborhood in which you grew up, or the shade of your beautiful skin, you are capable of any and everything you have ever dreamt of. When you know who you are and believe in who you are, you are a force that no one can stand up against. Never be easily swayed to do the things that are not authentic for you. A woman who knows who she is, is powerful. She is solid and unmoved in the foundation of who she is, yet fluid enough to adjust to the ebb and flow of life.

You have been created with all of the power, grace, love, and creativity you will need to make an impact on the lives of those around you. There is music in you – a sweet calling to create, to love, to learn, to grow, and to inspire.

Become a master of you – mastery of self is the greatest of all. Are you emotional or reactive? Do you feel things deeply? Or are you more of a thinker than a feeler? What are your strengths? What are your skills, gifts, or talents? What speaks to your soul? How do you view yourself or feel about yourself? Do you know what your purpose on this earth is? Do you know what purpose means?

No matter the chaos of the world around you, stand firm in your knowledge of self, in love, and in truth of who you are and all you have been created to be. Stand firm and unmoved in love, peace, faith, kindness, goodness, boldness, creativity, service to others, patience, forgiveness, healing, joy, and self-control.

You are gorgeous, smart, intelligent, capable, worthy of love and all of the greatest things you can imagine. There is a gift, a calling, a spirit in you. I want you equipped from the earliest of ages on knowledge of self, connection to your Creator, and in unconditional love. And when I say love, I don't mean the romantic kind. I mean that love from God, that love for yourself, that love of the life you have been blessed with – the love of everything in you and around you. I want to encourage you to walk in your greatness every single day – to operate in abundance, power, purpose, and peace. That dream, that plan, that purpose, and that calling inside of you can and will be manifested into fruition as you live in the authenticity of what speaks to your heart, your soul, and your spirit.

If it is not right for your body, your mind, your soul, or your spirit – if it is not serving your highest self or your greatest good, do not give yourself to it – boys, gossip, hate, fruitless friendships, etc. Your emotional and mental health are just as important as your physical health. And your spiritual health is most important. They all relate to the one another. Do what is right for you to take care of them all.

You may be someone who needs alone time to unwind. Whether you think you're an introvert or an extrovert, you have different ways of dealing with life and the energies around you. Do not compromise who you are for the comfort of others. If you need to heal, to write, to make music, to create art, to explore, to give your best in a sport, to meditate or spend time in silence.

Having the love and encouragement of our parents and surroundings is wonderful. It is great to be supported, loved, protected, and cared for. But this is about knowing all of those things exist already. No matter what you've been told, you already loved, protected, and cared for by your Creator. This Universe will conspire on your behalf as you put your best intentions out into the world. This is about standing firm in your truth without needing the acknowledgment of others – knowing that everything else is merely a bonus.

What if I were to tell you for 100 days straight that you were the most beautiful young woman in all of the world? Then on day 101, I didn't say anything to you at all. Would you question yourself? Or would you shrug it off and keep it moving knowing already that you are gorgeous, smart, and grounded?

What if I admired your art or your music or your athletic abilities or your writing – always giving you praise?

Then one day, I told you I hated everything about your work even after you've poured your heart into it and you know it is your best? Would you stop creating? Would you stop being who you are? I hope not.

What if your parents never told you how valuable your body, mind, heart, and time were? Then some popular, cute boy comes to tell you all of these things just to spend a little alone time with you doing the things he wants? Would you comply because what he's saying to you sounds good and fills a void? Are you willing to trade self-respect for attention?

This is why standing firm in your truth and having knowledge of self is so important to establish and maintain at a young age. You don't want to be confused, empty, used and abused, and scrambling to discover yourself when you're older. There are so many people in the world doing that very thing because it was not established or even explained to them early on. These people are hurting, desperate to be filled, empty, suffering, looking for something and someone to complete them. They are operating in dramas they've learned as children. These dramas are ways to manipulate for energy and attention from others because they never learned how to create this energy for themselves. God gives us his energy, love, and healing so freely, yet we are rarely taught how to tap into it. We are taught if we love people, buy things, make ourselves look and feel better, or strive in competition with others that we will somehow be complete. But, if only they would be still, they could awaken to the spirit of peace already within them. They could walk boldly in life rooted and grounded in who they are – unattached to the opinions and fickle feelings of others, expectations, labels, titles, and desired outcomes. We allow these things to destroy our peace, pull at our deepest emotions, and keep us stuck and unable to create our greatest works to display them for the world.

When you are inspired, you inspire others. When you stand firm in your foundation, you encourage the next man or woman to do the same. When you speak life over yourself and others, you don't wait around expecting anyone else to do it.

Your comfort and solace will never be found in anyone if you do not first find it in you. Never get into the habit of chasing temporary fillers. Temporary fillers are drugs, alcohol, lovers, attention, fruitless friendships, and unhealthy habits that temporarily make ourselves feel better only to destroy us later. Once that euphoric feeling wears off from one thing, we're on a desperate search for another.

We scroll social media, turn on the television, or walk down the street comparing ourselves to others. And for what? We think other women have more than we have. All the while, they may be looking at you feeling the same way.

When you know who you are and what you stand for, you are able to respect yourself and others. Because you care for your own being, you are able to care for others. If you have no knowledge of who you are, you are willing to do anything to yourself and others. You are willing to accept anything from anyone. That is not fruitful.

Be kind and gentle with yourself. Life is a journey, not a destination or a race. Do not fall for the programming and conditioning of what the perfect body looks like, or what path you're supposed to take. Knowing who you are is about being solid in yourself so that you cannot be swayed, bought, sold, or manipulated. Most of the chaos in the world around you is due to fear. We think that the opposite of love is hate, but it is fear — fear of lack, fear that what we have will be taken from us, fear of failure, fear of things unknown, fear that the people who look different from us will harm us in some way, fear of being hurt or let down: the list goes on. So many of us are searching and trying to find someone or something to complete us, medicate our pain, or make us feel better. This common practice comes from a misunderstanding of self and your value.

I always had so many feelings and emotions that I didn't know how to deal with or handle. I made terrible decisions with my body, my mind, my time, and my heart. And I want to assist you in skipping the 'dead space' or the 'lost years' so that you live out your days with great intention and power. I'm glad I made the decisions that I did – I had to gain every lesson from every experience. I am willing to be the martyr for you. I am willing to have gone through those things for you. All of those experiences brought me here to you – to pour out my heart and life lessons to empower you.

Learning to control your many confusing emotions is another way to gain knowledge of self. The actions and words of others may hurt you, but try not to take things personally. People can only deal with you as deeply as they've dealt with themselves. It is up to you and you alone to be the good in this world despite the foolery of others. Everyone won't always be nice and loving – things may hurt, sting, and embarrass you. But never let them devastate you. It is all about how you respond, how you react. Inner peace is the ultimate goal.

When you know who you are, you will understand you cannot control anything in this life. Everyone and everything changes. You must be able to roll with the punches and accept this truth. It will save you and your heart a world of unnecessary pain. The only thing you can control is how you react to life and what is brought your way – knowing that God gives us nothing that we cannot handle, knowing that you are fully capable to handle what is brought to you for you to grow and to learn and to ascend to your highest self.

Being made in the image of God means you have all of the power of the Divine within you. Created in his likeness equips you with a powerful creativity and wisdom. You are full of love, light, and peace. Joy, healing, and purpose are all found within you. Grab ahold of that power and never let it go. Walk boldly and without fear or doubt in the truth that you are amazing in every single way.

You cannot look to anyone to make you feel good about who you are. We are all conditioned from the day we are born to act, look, behave, be, feel, and think a certain way. And while most of these lessons are needed to function in society, some are less than ideal beliefs that cause us to question our authenticity.

Whether your parents are doctors and lawyers or high school graduates working a 9-5, know that you were born to them for a reason. The day you were born, the city in which you were born, the neighborhood in which you were raised – it's all for a greater purpose. You see, you must gain the experiences from your life in order to walk with understanding in your path. If your parents are the most incredible, loving, and supportive parents in the world. That is wonderful! Listen to their stories and their lessons. Be filled with their love and their wisdom. If your relationship is less than ideal, know that in that there is also a lesson.

What you do not get from them or friends or siblings, you can get from yourself. You can get from your God. You can get from this Universe that gives so freely of love and support. You must be grounded in you. No matter the background, each generation is meant to bring about a new level of being in this world. Take what you have learned from your parents and grandparents (both good and bad) and expound upon these things. Bring healing to yourself and past generations, break free from strongholds, and be fully who you are in this world.

There are many lessons I have learned and applied in my youth. But there are many more that I heard yet never listened to or that I never learned yet wished I had. Life is such a great gift, and I want to empower and equip you to live yours to the fullest.

True freedom comes from the freedom to be who we truly are. Don't stop yourself from being who you are to conform to the majority or the demands of society. You are a soul having a human experience. That soul is grounded in love and peace and the wisdom of the Divine. God is always present; He is everything and everywhere.

You're never too young or too old to have knowledge of self, to love yourself deeply, to understand and recognize the power of God within you, to love greatly, to walk in gratitude daily, and to arise to your purpose. Stay connected to Source. That love and energy is the same energy taking care of everything around you.

xoxo Brittni

Mindfulness

What is knowledge of self?

- Knowledge of Self is knowing and understanding the foundation of who you are – the essence and wisdom of your being.
- Knowledge of God – Source of all, the Creator, the Ultimate Healer, Lover, Forgiver, and Provider
- Knowledge of your gifts, talents, and abilities
- Knowledge of the impact you have in this world
- Knowledge of Spirit, Mind, Heart, and Body
- Knowledge of individuality
- Knowledge of the power of your mind
- Knowledge of being ground, rooted, and one with everything around you
- Knowledge of that you are a child/creation of God – a force to be reckoned with
- Knowledge of Self is about awareness. Bringing your thoughts, actions, words, and feelings into your conscious awareness to harness their love and power and use them to the highest benefit of Self and others

- Knowledge of Self is taking the time to understand you.

Before we can go out into the world and be our best, we must know who we are. Have you ever taken the time to truly know yourself? I mean, really figure out who you are and what you're made of? How can you be your best when you're questioning everything about yourself?

You were born for such a time as this. Who you are and what you have to offer is significant to the world around you. The day you were born, the precise minute you were born, the parents you were born to – every step has come to this moment. You have purpose. There is no coincidence in your being.

"You play the music that you came here to play, and God will help you overcome any obstacles or any struggles. It's not going to be a struggle, because God is supporting you."

– Wayne Dyer

Reflection

What do you love?

_____

_____

_____

_____

_____

_____

What do you dislike?

_____

_____

_____

_____

_____

_____

What brings you peace and purpose?

_____

_____

_____

_____

_____

_____

What or who takes it away?

_____

_____

_____

_____

_____

_____

What is the mark you want to leave on the world?

_____

_____

_____

_____

_____

What makes you, you?

_____

_____

_____

_____

_____

What brings you joy?

_____

_____

_____

_____

_____

_____

What drains your energy?

_____

_____

_____

_____

_____

_____

What excites you and makes you come alive?

_____

_____

_____

_____

_____

_____

What are your strengths?

_____

_____

_____

_____

_____

_____

What are some shortcomings or things you need to improve upon?

_____

_____

_____

_____

_____

_____

What is important to you?

_____

_____

_____

_____

_____

_____

Now, do me a favor. Head to the nearest mirror and look at yourself deep and hard. I think I've seen myself every single day for 27 years but never really looked at myself until recently. Look at your hands, your face, and those beautiful eyes – feel that love pour from your heart. You are greatness. You are made with love, light, and power.

CHAPTER TWO
Open Your Mind

Love, when I say 'open your mind', I mean just that. Now that you have a better knowledge of self, I want you to begin to open your mind and your heart to what is next in your life. Only those with open minds can begin to see the endless possibilities around and ahead of them. There is such a power in your thoughts, and the way you choose to experience the world around you will depend on your thoughts about yourself and your life. This new journey will begin in your mind, heart, and spirit. It has to.

When you are open-minded and believe you can change, change will be made possible. When you believe you are capable of expressing your art, you will notice creative expression begin to flow from you. Your mind is powerful. The biggest limits in your life will be the ones you create in your mind. You were created by a God with absolutely no limits – the power is yours. God and the angels are ready to go to work for you – they already believe in you. They're just waiting for you to open your mind, believe in yourself, put great thoughts out into the world, and wait for them to bring you the manifested results.

Have you ever heard the saying, Change your thoughts, change your life? Well it is true. When you begin to understand the power of your every thought, your every word, your ever action and feeling, then you will begin to embrace this energy. Your thoughts are energy forces. They emit a type of energy into the world around us and what aligns with that thought pattern is what will return to us. If you are always thinking negatively, you will begin to experience things, people, and situations that are negative.

Open your mind to new things, new experiences, seeing and traveling the world, conquering those fears and limitations, and being authentically you without shame. I want you to open your mind to letting go of old, outdated habits and establishing new ones that speak to your soul. I want you to open your mind to the world outside of your home, your street, your city, and even your state. I want you to open your mind to the places your talents and gifts can take you. I want you to open your mind to letting go of things and people who do not serve your highest good. I want you to open your mind to going on this journey to live your life purpose and soul mission. I want you to open your mind to perfecting your craft and learning new skills. I want you to open your mind to the way you act and react to unfavorable conditions. I want you to open your mind to love others regardless of their actions. I want you to open your mind to being a co-creator of your life. Open your mind to being a 'forever student' who is constantly learning and evolving. Open your mind to following the path you know is right for you. Open your mind going against what is widely accepted to do what is right and authentic to your journey.

We are fully co-creators with God. You are who you believe you are. You are all of the things God has said about you. He knew you and your greatness before your great-great-grandparents were even thought of. That is how powerful and ordained you are. Open your mind to that. Let that sink in. Put your trust and faith in that. You are a God-realized being, and when you open your mind to that, there is no limit to what you can create. All of the wisdom, light, power, and love that is within God and this world is also within you. He has created you for such a time as this! And as you open your mind to believe, you open your mind to create and to see things differently. When we hold onto negative thoughts, images, behaviors, and feelings, these are the things that are portrayed in our lives. If you think things are impossible, then, sweetheart, you are right. If you think you cannot heal, create, change, or move forward, then you will remain stagnant and complacent. If you accept a defeated way of living, then you will continue that pattern until you accept another way of being. If you think people are always out to get you or not to be trusted, you will attract people who prove you to be right.

Sometimes, we hold onto old thought patterns and ways of thinking because change threatens our comfort. But I will be the first to tell you that comfort is absolutely and in no way, shape, or form any friend of yours. When we change, we have to leave behind the old. Evolution is all about transcending to new levels of existence – this includes severing ties with every form of fear, doubt, negative thinking, and insecurity.

An open mind is needed to be able to transform into who you have been called to be. If we are to begin this transformation, we must open our minds and clear out what is burdening us. If we're going to go on this journey together, love, you must open your mind.

xoxo Brittni

Mindfulness

Opening your mind is one of the first steps to take in order to unlock your potential and power within. As you begin to open your mind, you make room for growth in all areas of your life. You make room for new outlooks, lessons, and experiences. Opening your mind allows you to unlearn what is old and outdated and make room for what is new and fresh. Life is about constantly evolving and shedding layers to reach your core. When you open your mind and reach your core, you are able to see the world through a new set of eyes. You cannot be close-minded and expect to grow in purpose and in truth.

The power of the mind and spirit brings about results and outcomes depending upon our focus of energy. You are free to change your mind at any time in order to connect to your ordained power.

To open your mind, let go of any preconceived notions that only what you know or believe is what is right. Come up with a daily spiritual practice to keep your mind free and open. It can be anything from walking in nature alone every morning to prayer or exercise. Mediation, affirmations, writing, creating your art, or just sitting in silence when you wake up are incredible ways of staying free and in the moment enough to keep your mind focused on the things that service your highest self.

Believe in the limitless possibilities of life and the world around you. Life is bigger than middle school or high school angst and dramas. Enjoy these years and embrace your youth, but know that you are more than just a student, a daughter, or a friend. You are bigger than what may have gone wrong or be going wrong right now (I hope that nothing is). You are more than your volleyball team. You are more than your grades. Open your mind to every incredible land, culture, world, country, language, accomplishment, goal, and possibility before you. Open your mind to the possibility of being a great person for yourself and others. Open your mind to traveling all across the globe – lying on the beaches of Fiji, learning the language of France, or dining on the cuisine in Italy. Open your mind to publishing your first book, hosting your first art show, or becoming a life-changing psychologist. Hold space for a life of peace, love, deep spirituality, gratitude, and exploration. Hold space for owning your own business or for studying abroad. Hold space for all things for there are absolutely no limits to you.

Reflection

Is your mind opened or closed?

_____

_____

_____

_____

_____

_____

If it is open, great! If not, do you want it to be?

_____

_____

_____

_____

_____

_____

What are your daily thoughts about yourself and your life?

_____

_____

_____

_____

_____

_____

Are these thoughts in alignment with the type of life you envision?

_____

_____

_____

_____

_____

_____

Are you carrying any limiting or negative thought patterns?
If so, what are they??

_____

_____

_____

_____

_____

_____

We are going to replace the negative with the positive and
begin our journey to replacing the old with the new. What
are the positive thought patterns you have about your life?
Who do you want to be??

_____

_____

_____

_____

_____

What are 5 things you want to accomplish, countries you want to see, or things you want to experience?

_____

_____

_____

_____

_____

_____

What are 5 spiritual practices that you can start doing each morning to ensure you stay in a positive headspace and stay open to greatness?

_____

_____

_____

_____

_____

_____

Create 3 positive affirmations that speak to you. An affirmation is a self-powering declaration that supports a positive mental attitude.

"I believe in the limitless possibilities of life."

"I am supported by my God-given talents, skills, and abilities to live a life of abundance."

_____

_____

_____

_____

_____

_____

_____

_____

_____

_____

_____

CHAPTER THREE
Unplug from False Agreements

Once we have examined ourselves and began to open our minds to new ways of existing, we must begin to unplug from the false agreements we have made with ourselves and the ones that may have been placed on us.

I remember being so emotional as a teenager. I felt everything so deeply – I still do. But being so young and unaware of myself, I occasionally acted or reacted in the wrong ways. My mom would jokingly call me bipolar. Now, bipolar disorder is real and nothing be joked about, but when my mother would say it to me, I would question whether or not what she was saying about me was true. I never claimed to be bipolar, but what she was saying made me feel badly about my deep emotions. I spent so many years trying not to feel so deeply just because I disliked being called 'emotional.' The tongue has the power to speak life or death over you and others – words have the power to penetrate and create self-limiting beliefs.

Have you ever been called a name or had a label placed on you so much that you started to believe it yourself? Have you ever been labeled a problem student? Or because you didn't excel in a certain class you thought you were not as smart as others who were being praised for acing their tests? What are some of the self-limiting beliefs that you have placed on yourself or others have placed on you?

Unplugging from false agreements is so crucial at this point in your life. An agreement is a term or condition that has been accepted. For example, if you scroll through social media and you see a certain body type being glorified, and you may compare your shape to theirs. Instead of knowing you are uniquely and perfectly made, you begin to accept that this is the only beautiful body type and label yourself as 'ugly' or 'unwanted' from that day forward. That is a false agreement you have made with yourself. Love your body the way it is. Love your skin the way it is. Love your hair the way it is. Stop hoping and wishing to be anyone but you. Love your mind, your heart, your laugh, your smile, your nose, your lips, your way of doing things just the way they are.

From every negative word you have said about yourself or someone has spoken to you – unplug right now. People do not understand the power of the words they speak over the lives of others, and when we do not know any better, we begin to internalize these things. When you attach yourself to false agreements, you're more vulnerable to the negative thoughts, actions, and ways of living.

I once told some family members that I wanted to write full-time, travel the world, guide individuals towards their purpose, and mentor creative youth. Instead of encouraging this, they immediately questioned me wanting to thrive on my own and work for myself. They felt it would be safer to stay in the corporate world with benefits and a "guaranteed" paycheck. I could have internalized that and accepted what they thought was sound advice. But, I chose not to agree with those limitations and believe in what I knew was the calling on my life. I refused to make a false agreement.

We must take ownership over our lives. How will you be your best self and prosper in this world carrying the weight of false agreements around with you? How can you be free and experience happiness and joy when accepting the limits that others have placed on you?

Save yourself some trouble and understand right now in your youth that when people say things that are hurtful or discouraging, they are only dealing with you from their levels of thinking and understanding. It is nothing personal against you. People can only deal with you as deeply as they have dealt with themselves. Brush empty or lifeless words off and keep it moving. When you know who you are, you smile in the faces of those who tell you something is impossible to achieve.

Build your life on solid ground so that you are unmoved in times of trouble. Understand that with life, trials will come. That is just a part of life. But, you have been equipped to overcome. If you are grounded and rooted in this wisdom, discernment, truth, love, peace, and goodness, you will be able to face trouble and get through it without allowing it to consume you.

Love your body the way it is. Love your skin the way it is. Love your hair the way it is. Stop hoping and wishing to be anyone but you. Love your mind, your heart, your laugh, your smile, your nose, your lips, your way of doing things just the way they are.

One by one, we can sever ties with limits and conditioning. As we begin the change within ourselves, so will the change be realized in our external worlds. Our conditioning and false agreements limit our potential. As we begin to unplug from things that do not resonate with our highest selves, we are able to birth new life and a new way of thinking. We break up with hurt, pain, fear, doubt, and limitations to embrace life, love, abundance, power, purpose, peace, and a thriving existence. Trust fully in the Divine source within you and live with incredible intention.

As we change and unplug with lack and limits, we inspire others to do the same. The change begins with us. As we live our truths and vibe on higher levels, we encourage others to speak and live theirs. As we claim our paths of purpose and meaningful goals, we give way for others to awaken to their own soul missions. Making a commitment to love and nurture yourself is a true inspiration to yourself and anyone who is witness to the new you. There is nothing wrong with loving yourself, knowing the truth about you, and refusing to let others dim your light.

To do what is right and authentic, we must let go of what is fake and burdensome. You have the permission to unplug from the wrong ways of thinking and feeling about yourself. You have permission to thrive, to love wholeheartedly, to live unashamedly, and to allow your gifts, talents, and skills to speak for you. Unplugging from mediocrity, low expectations, social constraints and conditioning, fear, lack mentality, old habits, wrong agreements, and people/things that no longer serve you is an act of empowerment!

It is time for change and transformation! Focus on what you do want instead of focusing your vital life force energy on the things less desirable or that others limit you to. Develop positive agreements and beliefs about yourself and the beautiful world around you. What you give energy to is what will manifest. So keep your eyes, feelings, and thoughts on abundance and not lack. As I have already explained to you, you are the co-creator of your life. Your words, thoughts, feelings, and actions have great power, so only think and speak positively over your life. Take responsibility for you – it is not too early to live your best life.

xoxo Brittni

Mindfulness

What you believe and accept about yourself contributes to how you walk, talk, think, and act. If you agree to limits, negative self-images, and self-deprecating thoughts then you put a cap on yourself. You keep yourself from being who you are. You limit yourself when you were never created to be limited or held back in any way.

Keep everyone's false agreements out of your head. If you hear them, dismiss them and brush them off immediately. Do not internalize the personal problems of others. Keep this in mind when others say negative things, call your names, or attempt to limit your being or ambition in any way. These types of people are merely projecting their own internal issues on you. They look at themselves and have to question why they aren't thriving and why you think you have the audacity to believe you can. To understand this in your youth will save yourself so much confusion and many hurt feelings.

This is why knowledge of self, an open mind, and creating powerful agreements about yourself will benefit you now rather than later. This keeps you from having to heal from your childhood. This keeps you from settling for whatever and whomever does not serve your highest self.

This keeps you from the lost years and dead space of confusion. This creates the solid foundation to build upon. This opens space for love and purpose. When we respond to the call on our lives, we do not have time for unruly emotions and false agreements for our energy is focused on our greatness.

In a society that praises scripted false selves and copies, have the courage to be authentic and original. Be proud and enthusiastic about who you are. Black Girl, you are the epitome of grace, poise, beauty, and excellence. You are the stars and the cosmos, the sun and the moon. Your mind, body, and soul are to be respected and taken care of. Act as such.

Reflection

What are some false agreements you've allowed others to attach to you or that you may have made for yourself?

1. _____

_____

2. _____

_____

3. _____

_____

4. _____

_____

5. _____

_____

6. _____

_____

7. _____

_____

8. _____

_____

9. _____

_____

10. _____

_____

I want you to look at those false agreements and understand that not one of those limiting agreements belongs to you. We are shifting our focus to what serves us – the truth of our existence. Sever ties with every single negative, limiting thought you've had about yourself.

Now, let's make 10 new agreements about yourself and your new path.

1. _____

_____

2. _____

_____

3. _____

_____

4. _____

_____

5. _____

_____

6. _____

_____

7. _____

_____

8. _____

_____

9. _____

_____

10. _____

_____

Read these aloud, write them out on index cards to carry with you, or just say them silently in your head to yourself with conviction. These are your truths. We will transform and evolve into the women we are and break up with the anything that does not support that evolution.

CHAPTER FOUR
Authenticity: True Self

When I speak of authenticity, I speak of your truest self and spirit. Being authentic is the act of letting go of who we think we're supposed to be and embracing who we are. Authenticity is about removing the masks and facades we have learned to portray. In order to be who we truly in this world, you must awaken to your highest self and shed what is false and unreal. To awaken to your highest self, you must be authentic in your words and actions.

To be authentic, we must let go of our ego-based teachings and daily practices to embrace the spirit of our true selves. The transformation from ego to true self is an important one if we are to evolve and grow in our spiritual gifts. Shedding the old and outdated habits of the ego allows you to sever ties with this false self you've grown so accustomed to. Authenticity allows for love-based living and is truly about being real, transparent, and visible. This gives us freedom from fear. In this new-found freedom, we are able to align with the reality of love and the power within.

"The authentic self is the soul made visible."

– Sarah Ban Breathnach

Ego vs. True Self	
Fear-based	Love-based
Me	We
Looks to be filled by others	Whole on your own
Arrogant	Humble
Lack	Abundance
Narrow-minded	Open-minded
Selfish & Self-Centered	Selfless
Drawn to lust	Drawn to love
Unforgiveness	Forgiving
Serves itself	Serves others
Gossiping & Petty	Speaks life into others
Competition	Understands there is room for all

Seeks wisdom	Understands the soul *is* wisdom
Enjoys the prize	Enjoys the journey
Looks outward	Looks inward
Cause of pain	Cause of healing

The ego operates in a fear-based external world. It is in constant struggle and angst. It has the need to be accepted and is in constant fear of losing something. The ego operates in a "me" mentality – meaning it is selfish and self-centered. Ego is always a victim of circumstance. When we operate in these lower level energy ways of living, we are operating in learned and observed practices that we feel we need to get by in this world. This is simply not true. Look around: has it gotten us anywhere?

True self operates in a love-based internal world. True self is in harmony with itself and the world around it. The authentic, true self operates in abundance knowing there is always enough. Spirit seeks to serve others and uses its gifts for the empowerment of humanity. True self loves and appreciates life as a gift. True self operates in love, patience, peace, letting go, unity, gratitude, sympathy, and empathy. The authentic self is open-minded and is willing to embrace change and evolve.

To see the true beauty of your gifts, your art must come from the heart, the soul, and a spirit of authenticity. Living authentically in your truths and gifts is an inner experience. Your authentic self knows it is an artist made of infinite energy and resource. This is the realm of our greatness in which we must operate deeply and fully. Our lives and our gifts must live from the inside out. When we are one with Spirit, our God-given gifts are able to be realized and our purpose brought into fruition.

Are your current thoughts, actions, and words in alignment with the vision you have for your life? If they are not, how can we change this? As we awaken to true self, life is still going to go on around us. It is our responsibility to take what we have learned and live it fully with great intention. When the world calls you, and it will, you must be able to listen inwardly and honor your spiritual being. We must not allow friends, family, peers, media, or social traditions to pull at us so forcefully that we cease to operate in the truth of who we are. We must be willing to do the work and put in the time. Once we learn how to be true to ourselves in this world, it is our duty to live and practice these truths every single day. With practice, these habits will take the place of the old, outdated habits. We will watch our external worlds change due to the internal work.

You are spirit before you are body, created and manifested for a reason. You have a calling and purpose on your life, and it is time to be exactly who you are and have always been in order to see your gifts used to their fullest potential. You are a soul, a spirit having a human experience; you must nurture your soul and water it daily. To water your soul daily, find quiet time to pray, meditate, exercise, journal, or just walk silently in nature. Take the time to keep your soul grounded in love and peace, so that you may walk without shame in your truths.

xoxo Brittni

Mindfulness

Gaining knowledge of self, embracing an open mind, and creating agreements that serve us make room for a life of authenticity. Living an authentic life brings clarity and freedom. It allows us to be who we are without shame, fear, or care for society's ridiculous standards. You know there is something incredible about you – so feel it and walk in it. Let us see your soul. Let us hear what you have to stay. Let go of the unnecessary burdens you have been carrying. Let that peace be ushered in. Let us be encouraged by your spirit and your art. The joy and truth of your inner world will shine through and manifest into your outer world.

Embrace your true nature. Take that mask off. Hopefully, I've caught you before you have even put one on. I was a teenage girl once. You turn on the tv or scroll through social media and you're told how to look, what is attractive and what isn't, and what's an acceptable way to act. You're taught that makeup is better than your beautiful face. You're to gossip, to grow up too fast, to give your body away to whomever gives you the slightest bit of attention, to be popular or crave the approval and attention of your peers. You've been programmed to admire celebrities and model your life based on the fake reality of reality television. There are so many things that you are exposed to, but rarely is life spoken into you.

Authentic living allows you freedom from all of the nonsense and constant noise. It allows you the space to be your highest self. It allows you to vibrate so high that toxic people and ideals no longer affect your life. Authentic living as your true self sets you free. It allows you to serve others and see your life as a gift. Your soul must be nourished. In this, your soul will feel abundance instead of lack. You will enjoy and embrace the journey of life's ups and downs. Your soul will embrace God, his unlimited love for you, and the calling he's had on your life since before your parents named you. Your true nature is drawn to unconditional love, wisdom, and wholeness. Look inward before searching around for anyone or anything to validate you. You are already enough. You are whole. You are capable.

Reflection

Have you been living authentically? Or, have you been living an ego-based life filled with the wrong thoughts, actions, and reactions?

_____

_____

_____

_____

_____

_____

We've learned that ego serves itself. It seeks outward recognition and a life of constant competition with others. Ego looks outward before inward. Ego feels lack and seeks to cause pain. Living an ego-based life seeks for others to fill us instead of knowing we are whole on our own.

Name 5 ways you act or react in ego on a regular basis:

1. _____

_____

2. _____

_____

3. _____

_____

4. _____

_____

5. _____

_____

Authentic, soul living is important on our journey. It is who we are in our purest form. It allows us to walk in our purpose and passion with clarity and love for our work. It allows us to create our best work and art. This life is a gift. Embrace it.

Name 5 ways to describe your true and authentic self:

1. _____

_____

_____

2. _____

_____

_____

3. _____

_____

_____

4. _____

_____

_____

5. _____

_____

_____

Spend time watering your soul and your authentic self through meditation, clean eating, exercising, journaling, or whatever speaks to you. What are 3 practices that speak to you?

1. _____

   _____

   _____

2. _____

   _____

   _____

3. _____

   _____

   _____

CHAPTER FIVE
Gifts, Talents, and Skills

Dear Talented Soul,

There is no coincidence or chance in your existence. You have been equipped with talents and abilities that are just for you. These talents, skills, and gifts are to be used to their utmost potential for the manifestation of purpose and joy in your life and the lives of others. Live and fulfill these things with optimism, enthusiasm, and power. Your gifts and talents will make a way for you. Believe in them. Believe in you. If you don't and you allow those talents to lay dormant, those who need you will go without what you have to give. My love, don't let this be you.

For me, writing gives me life. There's something about the ability to use words in such a way to tell stories, to cleanse and bring healing, to inspire, and to encourage. I've been writing since I was six-years-old, and it always came so naturally. Any chance I got to write, I did. I would pour my heart and soul onto a piece of paper better than I could express anything verbally. My mind and imagination were so vivid and my heart was so full. I was born to write – and for a myriad of reasons. I pulled inspiration from journaling, theater, and 300-page novels. I would get lost in stories and always wrote about things that meant a great deal to me. It was so fulfilling, fun, and therapeutic.

I know so many of you feel the same way about your art, your music, your gifts and abilities. I understand the rush you get when you pick up that paint brush and pour your soul onto the canvas. I understand fully how it feels to have words bubble up inside of you to the point where you have no option but to write and keep on writing. Even in your sports, the way you play and put in hours of practice. There is so much beauty in the gifts, talents, skills, and abilities that you have. I am inspired by you, and so is everyone watching. We need you. We need to see your commitment, your natural talent, and your skill.

Step into your personal power and embrace those gifts. Activate that black girl magic and have faith in your abilities. When you do, you allow greatness to flow from you. Trust in all you have to give of yourself and to this world. Believe fully in your skills and gifts. Use them to their highest potential. Be grateful for them and the purpose they hold. From sports to arts to doctoral degrees, from the gift of healing and transforming to the ability to encourage and inspire, your skills are unique and purposeful.

Take a second to breathe in the wonders of you. Use this moment to open your mind to all of the lives you will change and all of the places you will go. Nothing is holding you back. Nothing is keeping you from what God has already claimed over your life. These gifts, talents, and abilities were given to you well before your parents even knew you would exist. These things were already placed within you for a purpose greater than yourself. Let yourself be used to fulfill what needs to be changed, loved, and fulfilled in our life experience. The world needs more and more people like you. The talents, gifts, and skills you have create flames that ignite other beautiful minds. Those who seek self-enlightenment, illumination, and empowerment need your light.

Use your talents and abilities to serve humanity. Use them to bring joy, peace, clarity, and meaning to your life and the lives of those in your community. Be the change and exceptional gifts you want to see in this world. Exercise your talents with commitment, dedication, and love. Put your soul into your work. Your gifts will make a way for you. They were given to you for such a time as this. There is a Divine plan and calling on your soul. Do what you have come here to do. Your drive and dedication to your skills will cause others who are watching to see and to want to do the same. Walk in the Divine calling on your soul.

Xoxo Brittni

Mindfulness

What we do with our talents, skills, and gifts is so important. We're all a part of the ebb and flow of the world around us. When we give freely of our gifts, we contribute to that ebb and flow and contribute this life experience. Some of us are natural writers, artists, and speakers. Others were born to be the doctors, lawyers, or teachers. Many of us were put here to heal, love, encourage, and inspire. There is a calling within you, and you are fully equipped with everything you need to bring your plans and goals into fruition by using the gifts God has given you.

Our gifts and talents are not always job- or occupation-related. If you're a healer, you can heal with your words and actions on a daily basis. If your mission is to show this world that love will always conquer over fear, then let the world see unconditional love through you. It may not be what you do to make money – it may simply just be who you are. Some of us most certainly want to use our natural gifts to provide a service to the world that we can turn into a way to earn income and free up our time for our families, travel, and things we love. But it is not the only way to serve humanity and be fulfilled.

●●●

What are the differences in talents, gifts, and skills?

Talent – a natural ability you were born with, but not
necessarily for Divine purpose

Gift – a natural capacity from God for Divine purpose

Skill – a learned area of expertise that you acquire

As you can see, they are all pretty similar with slight
differences. Talents and Gifts are both natural, but Gifts
propel you into your purpose where Talents are great
abilities to possess. Skills are slightly different as they may
not come naturally to you, but can be learned and executed
well with practice and experience.

Trust in the power of your skills; in the heart of your
talents and gifts. It is amazing and mind-blowing that
before our parents even knew our names, God had already
called us for more. He didn't say we needed degrees and

certificates to define us. There are already talents and gifts he has placed within us for a purpose greater than ourselves. Degrees, certificates, and accolades only enhance that which is already apart of who we are. Our hearts are filled with purpose and passion.

Talents and gifts are things that come naturally to you. Most of the time you naturally excel in the area of your talent. Mine has always been writing. Writing may be a learned skill, but for those of us who know what it feels like to truly write from the heart, we are able to embrace it is a natural gift. It has been a tug in us from the start. You can also excel in the area of a learned skill. For you, these skills can range from writing to problem-solving, from cooking to mentoring. Each of you were born with something you have the ability to do and do well. It is up to you to embrace that gift and follow the path of your talents and strengths.

Be intentional with your abilities – natural or learned. You must be your talents, gifts, and skills, to action. You can be the greatest writer and philosopher, but if you never produce any work or go long periods without being productive, it can be harder and harder to maximize these skills. For me, it took some time getting back in the groove after taking a lot of time off from writing. When this book came to me, I had to get back into the groove of writing consistently.

The world needs what you have. I've already said this and will continue to do so. Use that creativity to inspire, to heal, to release, to create, and to love. Be a change agent. Be bold in your talents and perfect that ability – always learning and continuing to grow in it. Love it and learn it.

We are the leaders, the teachers, the healers, the talented, the gifted, the skilled, and the called. Let us thrive and walk boldly in our abilities!

Reflection

What are my natural talents?

_____

_____

_____

_____

_____

_____

What are the skills that I have learned and now excel in?

_____

_____

_____

_____

_____

_____

In what areas do you find yourself to be the most gifted?

_____

_____

_____

_____

_____

_____

How can I use my gifts to serve humanity and make a positive difference in the world??

_____

_____

_____

_____

_____

CHAPTER SIX
What Makes Your Heart Sing?

I woke up this Saturday morning thinking about you. I got dressed, headed downtown to my favorite Starbucks location, pulled out my laptop and got to work. I love the smell of fresh coffee on a Saturday morning. I love watching women catch up with their friends, men sitting in cushioned chairs sipping their drink of choice while reading their chosen novel of the week, and I love the sound of typing on my laptop.

There were so many things on my mind, and I didn't know where to start. The first question that popped into my head was: Why spend one more second doing anything that doesn't make your heart sing? I ask myself this question from time to time and wish I had asked it more when I was your age. I'm sure it would have saved me so much time and confusion.

What makes your heart sing brings you joy, opens your mind to opportunities, and cultivates the energy to manifest; it speaks to your soul, individuality, and authenticity. It helps you to focus, to love fully, and to recharge. When we make time for things that speak to our hearts, we open up to creative expression.

I love things that bring me joy and things that will bring help, love, happiness, and laughter to others. I love doing things that are important to me and things that resonate with a cause that I'm passionate about. We weren't meant to just work for 60 years to retire. We weren't meant to just sleep, eat, and watch television all day. We were meant for so much more. There is so much life inside of you.

What are you passionate about? What makes your heart sing? All of our answers will be different, and that is the beauty of life. We all have our own interests, hobbies, and things we are passionate about. What sets our souls ablaze helps us to express the truth of who we really are and allows us to share our creativity and authenticity with the world. Do you like taking a morning run or going for a daily swim? Maybe you like yoga and meditation. Or maybe dance and ballet are your things? Are you a dancer, an artist, a lover, or a healer? Are your days spent in the theater working on your latest play? Whatever your thing is, practice it as often as you can. When we practice what brings us joy, we hold space for our energy to be illuminated. When we are full of joy, it is easier for greater things to flow to us. When we do what we love, we make room for abundance to flow freely into our life experiences.

The things that bring us joy help make us who we are. And when we do what feels right to our highest selves, we let go of limits and are able to be uplifted in so many ways. Our passions make room for self-love and self-care. They make room for creative expression and release. They make room for freedom. We need time for the things and people that make us happy. We need time for music, museums, barefoot walks in the grass, and cups of coffee snuggled up in bed with our favorite book. We need time for infectious laughter and days at the beach. We need rest, hot baths, and alone time for reflection. We need these things for our peace and mental sanity. We need these things for our hearts and to take full advantage of recharging our vital life force energy. When you are in a space of enthusiasm, love, and genuine zeal for life, you are connected with the heart of the Universe. When you are riding the wave of that awesome energy, it is easy for you to see the limitless possibilities for your life. You are able to create and manifest incredible things.

The things that make our hearts sing hold space for healing, transformation, evolution, light, love, and new life. They hold space for the clarity needed to create our best work. They allow us to be authentic in a world full of distractions. We must define the things that make our hearts sing, then do these things as often as we can.

Xoxo Brittni

Mindfulness

What makes your heart sing and brings your joy has so much to do with the calling on your life. Acknowledge the things that make your heart sing, then set aside the time to for them. If you don't you'll become depleted as you fall into the routine of life. We need activities, hobbies, and outlets that allow us to do the things we are passionate about. This allows us to generate our own happiness, joy, and peace from within. This helps you hone in on the energy that will feed your talents, gifts, and individuality.

Life is ready for you – for you to live. When you are consumed with the joy of things that speak to you, you are able to produce your best work. When we are able to give our all to our work, we are living to our fullest potential. This is all about living a genuine life, about original, free, and authentic. These lessons you learn now will carry you far in life. You will learn more lessons and expand upon what you feel is right for you.

That creative, loving, beautiful, and powerful energy within you is such an incredible gift. There are so many avenues to enjoy this life. There is no limit to the ways you experience this life or this world. Because there are no limits to your God, there are no limits to you. He knew when He created you what would be exciting and fulfilling to you. He knew what would speak to you and your individuality. He knew what would spark your interest and inspire you to get the job done. Have fun in those things. Enjoy this life experience with great enthusiasm and bliss.

Reflection

What makes your soul happy and your heart sing?

_____

_____

_____

_____

_____

_____

What do you love to do?

_____

_____

_____

_____

_____

_____

What do you love about yourself most?

_____

_____

_____

_____

_____

_____

Who or what inspires you?

_____

_____

_____

_____

_____

_____

Are you happy with the direction in which your life is headed? Why or why not?

_____

_____

_____

_____

_____

_____

What brings you true joy?

_____

_____

_____

_____

_____

_____

What are you most passionate about?

_____

_____

_____

_____

_____

_____

What is important to you?

_____

_____

_____

_____

_____

_____

_____

How can you pursue these things and incorporate them into your daily life?

_____

_____

_____

_____

_____

_____

_____

_____

_____

_____

_____

CHAPTER SEVEN
Foster Your Talents and Master Your Craft

I remember scrolling through social media a few days ago and running across a video of this young girl singing. She stood at a piano being played by her instructor. Her hair was pulled up into a scarf, and she was belting her rendition of Rihanna's "Man Down" as the teacher played the keys. She couldn't have been more than 16 years old, but the depth and power in her voice sent chills up my spine. It was such an incredible experience, and I felt it deep within my soul. In that moment, I began to think about you. I could feel each and every one of you – those who can sing, those who can dance, those who can draw, and those who can design. I felt those of you who engineer, invent, write code, or find cures. I could feel each of every one of you who stand up for a cause or change their community. Images flashed before me of those of you who want to be the first in their families to move out of the old neighborhood and travel the world or get a degree. I could feel you all and the incredible talent and passion within you.

The feeling I felt when I heard that young girl sing is the same feeling you will incite in others when they see or hear your work. That is what all of our greatness is all about. We change, we inspire, we encourage, and we empower. We love, we help, we heal, and we serve humanity with our talents. When you are equipped with impeccable skills, you must foster those talents and gifts within you. Those talents and skills must be developed and our crafts mastered. You must find the place inside of you where nothing is impossible and give your talents and crafts the attention and love they deserve. The more you work on you, the more you'll produce, publish, and share your talents with the world. The more art we have to look at, the more words we have to read, the more cures we have for diseases, the more solutions we have for our problems, the more we will make this world an even greater place.

To foster talents is to nurture them. When you nurture something, you care for it, you spend time with it, and you encourage its growth. It also means you can't waste your time on things that don't matter, that don't nurture your calling, that don't add light to the world. Rather, you put in the time to develop your talents and master them with training, experience, and expression. This is what you must do with your talents and crafts. Work on them and develop them in such a way that you are a force to be reckoned with. Give them the gentle love and attention that they deserve.

You are the next generation of leaders, dreamers, doers, movers, and shakers. Align yourself with the power of your talents and set aside the time to perfect them. Take a class, practice your skills, and learn more about who you are and what you do. Reject mediocrity, fear, and doubt as you focus your energy on what is more than possible for your life. Never apologize for your greatness. Share it and shout it from the rooftops. For your greatness and your mastered crafts will change the world and inspire others to awaken to their own abilities. Keep getting better and growing in your art. Keep dancing, keep healing, keep learning, and keep going. You lack nothing, for God has equipped you with everything.

Xoxo Brittni

Mindfulness

To foster means to promote, encourage, and cultivate. You must cultivate and encourage your abilities in order for them to reach their full potential. You may be talented in a sport or skill, but if you never put this skill to use, then what is the impact? Yes, you may be gifted, but hard work and intentional action conquers all.

How do we do these things, you ask?

1. Align: Make a decision to foster your talents and reject mediocrity; align yourself with your gifts, talents, and natural skills. Center yourself with the authenticity of being true to who you are and what you're capable of bringing to the world. You are being called to dive deeply into raw, vulnerable, inspired, and loving creativity. Let go of the burdens, false expectations, and facades of living a life with no intention.

2. Set Aside Time: The same time you set aside for other things that do not matter, put into those things that speak to your soul. If singing makes you happy, or writing, counseling, healing, being an advocate, mentoring, running successful board

meetings, writing music, film, dance, theater, (my list could go on forever) – there should be a significant amount of time put into watering these talents for growth. Write for 20 minutes each day. Write new lyrics for your song. Work on your blog or website. Get started on the screenplay. Get in front of the mirror and work on those new dance moves. Whatever 'it' is for you, give it your time, attention, and devotion.

3. Perfect Your Skills: Take a class. Teach a class. Offer your assistance to someone for free. Continue to learn more and more about your skills and how to develop them. The more you practice and learn, the better the content.

Nurture and foster your gifts. They are unique and to be honored. When we reject those authentic parts of ourselves, we wind up unfulfilled, upset, irritable, and watching as time passes us by. Let us foster our talents and reject mediocrity. Let us live lives of love, power, and intention.

Love and cultivate your talents. Be bold and unashamed. Sing your songs and write your words. Explore this world and all of its wonders. You are talented and supported. You have permission to be the greatest, most authentic version of you.

Let the world feel you. We're ready.

Reflection

How can you foster your talents and work daily (and realistically) to perfect your abilities?

_____

_____

_____

_____

_____

_____

What motivates you to reject mediocrity in your abilities?

_____

_____

_____

_____

_____

_____

What else can you learn about your craft or field of interest?

_____

_____

_____

_____

_____

_____

What can you do on a daily basis to put your abilities to work?

_____

_____

_____

_____

_____

CHAPTER EIGHT
Making the Decision to Engage the Process

Dear Creative Spirit,

When you make the decision to engage the process and the journey, this action sets off a force of motion that conspires on your behalf. To engage the process means you acknowledge the new awareness you have created about yourself and your life, and you are choosing to walk in your new path with enthusiasm, vigor, and clarity. You may have a calling on your life, but you still must choose to act. You have been called because you are capable and have something to give, but you have to take intentional, positive steps towards the goal. This physical world is malleable, and your experiences will change once you shift your attention and focus to engage in the process. Make a decision to live with an open-mind and heart in this world. Make a decision to do what it takes to get from where you are to where you want and need to be.

Engaging the process means to be aware and active in your life and the decisions you make on this journey. Life is a process and a gift. Love your life and make every ordained breath a purposeful one. Using your gifts to serve humanity is a process. Choosing to accept yourself, embrace yourself, and be the best person you can be on a daily basis is a process. When we engage these processes, we are raising awareness to become intentional in our words, thoughts, feelings, and actions. We are committed to our lives and the types of experiences we want to create. We engage the process by keeping our mind open to the journey of life and all it has to offer, knowing and understanding that it is not a race. We are not here to compete with anyone. Be committed to the process, but fluid enough to go with the flow.

It does not have to take you 27 years to move through confusion, bad decisions, and dead space. Your change can happen right now. Just make the decision to engage the process. It won't always be easy, but it will be worth it. Life is a powerful process. It demands knowledge, inner-wisdom, and the highs and lows of human nature. We must be open to understanding the nature of this experience.

When we turn on the news or look to social media and see young black women breaking barriers, kicking down doors, and creating their own lanes, it should fan the flame burning within each of us. These young women have chosen to embrace life, make decisions that are authentic to them, and engage the process of the journey they have taken.

As you move from the old you to make room for this new empowered you, things will begin to manifest and make sense. It is the time to smile and act. All you have to do is say, "Yes." The positive, productive energies around you will hear you and respond with great action. When you take one step, God will take ten. I promise you that.

The process will cause you to learn, evolve, grow, and unlearn that which no longer serves you. Having the patience to accept the process and the perfect timing of how things will unfold is a small part of the larger picture. To live at our highest potential, we must make a decision to be our highest selves. It will take that higher energy, focus, clarity, and inner-wisdom to succeed. It will take the activation of that black girl magic and the strength of that deep heritage from your ancestors.

Xoxo Brittni

Mindfulness

When it comes to your life, your purpose, and your passions, engaging the process is crucial to your success. To engage the process, you must become fully aware of your actions, then fully involved in the journey of your life. For us to live authentic lives, we must be intentional and purposeful in our participation with the plan and the path. This path is not about perfection; it is about purpose. It is about doing your best and giving this life your all. You were created with greatness already within you. Once you combine that greatness and those gifts with intentional engagement, you are able to love, serve, and reach lives you're meant to impact. Engaging the process is about setting sail, knowing that you are fully supported on this journey. You must trust yourself and your inner-wisdom to be your guide. There is no flaw in God's plans for you. Follow His guidance and His lead.

Once you say, "Yes!," to what is for you, you'll notice things, people, and experiences begin to align for you, ushering you in the right direction. Follow that. It will lead you where you need to be. The day I decided to write this book and start a non-profit organization for creatives in the next generation, everything and everyone I needed began to align with my decision.

Listen to those thoughts and urges you get to move forward in your schoolwork, your gifts and talents, and your purpose. Trust and believe in yourself and your ability to see these things through. Take the appropriate actions as you are guided. You will be incredible in all that you do. You are amazing and capable. Step out of your comfort zone and into greatness. Follow the path of your true desires and let God handle the details. Your desired outcome is more than possible.

This path will require work, dedication, passion, discipline, and time. But it will be worth it. If you need help, reach out to a trusted teacher, mentor, or friend. Pray for guidance, and it will be given to you. Take positive, intentional action in the direction of your dreams, plans, and goals. Have a love-infused positive attitude toward your life purpose and soul mission. Engage yourself in activities that are steps toward your goals. Stay optimistic about the magic inside of you, a magic that creates new worlds and opens new doors. Opportunities will present themselves to you on this path. You have a chance to create the life you desire, and your needs will be met as you move in the direction of your desired outcome.

Engage in the process – let nothing and no one keep you from it.

Reflection

What is the best first step you can take to engage the process?

_____

_____

_____

_____

_____

_____

What positive actions will you take toward your goals?

_____

_____

_____

_____

_____

_____

How will you step out of your comfort zone?

_____

_____

_____

_____

_____

_____

_____

Who can you use in your support network to hold you accountable?

_____

_____

_____

_____

_____

When you feel discouraged on your path, what are some ways you can shift your thinking to keep going?

_____

_____

_____

_____

_____

CHAPTER NINE
Vision, Values, and Goals

On January 1st of the last 3 years, I wake up early, head to the living room to my stack of previously collected magazines, and pop open a bottle of my favorite champagne. I make a comfortable space for myself, my 'zines, and my posters/supplies on the floor; then, I begin to get my vision on. I know a lot of people who you use vision boards yearly, monthly, and even weekly. They work for me, and I love them. You won't even imagine the things, trips, and people who have come into my life just by me simply knowing what I wanted and visualizing those things coming to me. Every picture, every word, and every phrase that I cut out and glue onto my board is authentic to me and the vision I have for my year. They are the things I want to see come into fruition, the trips I want to manifest, and the actions I need to take to get me from where I am to where I want to be. My entire trip to Fiji was manifested by visualizing and making that vision plain on my board.

But you don't have to use a board to define your vision. What you need is to understand your values, use your values to pair with your vision, and to put those value-based visions down on paper or whatever physical form works for you. Establishing values at your age is crucial for your decision-making process. It is never too early to define your values.

To have a clear vision for your ideal life, you must first focus on your values. Defining your values and what is important to you helps you to create a values-based vision that is more authentic and speaks to you and your unique life experience. Values are what you deem important in your life – your principles or standards of behavior. Some value achievement, wealth, and family. While others value integrity, service, and abundance. I, for example, value travel, peace, and financial independence. So, when I visualize and put my vision to paper, I am more likely to make decisions based on these values. Travel is important to me, so I make sure I visualize a year with multiple domestic and international trips. I value peace, so I tend to prefer situations and a line of work that will cultivate a spirit of peace and calm in life. I value financial independence and using my gifts to make a way for me, so I transitioned out of the corporate world into entrepreneurship.

Once you have defined your values, you are able to create an overall vision for your life and your life's work. Your vision for your ideal life is going to be helpful for breaking down your long-term goals into short-term, tangible, and measurable goals. Your vision needs to be something you are passionate about and dedicated to. If it isn't, nothing will motivate you to fulfill it. A vision based on values will help you to check yourself when it comes to actions, words, and/or thoughts that are not in alignment with the vision.

A life vision without defined values will look something like this: I want to achieve my dreams, get married, and live in another country. My ideal work is coaching. My ideal place to live is Europe. My ideal lifestyle is a thirty-hour work week with enough spare time to spend with my husband.

Yes, that's a goal. But it is broad, unenthusiastic, and honestly, pretty boring.

A life vision with defined values will look something like this: I will live authentically, spiritually, and wholly with God so that I am able to fulfill my life purpose and soul mission. I am using my natural skills, talents, and abilities in writing, mentoring, and life purpose inspiration to contribute to creative-minded youth, life purpose clients, and the overall growth of society. I am traveling the world and learning new languages while I experience new cultures and lands – hopefully impacting them as positively as I would have them to impact me. I am sharing my life with my loving, supportive, and adventurous partner while we live abundantly in Venice, Italy and cultivate an environment for a strong and healthy marriage. My ideal place to live is Venice, Italy; my ideal work is self-employed life purpose coach and published, best-selling author generating income by using my gifts as a service to humanity. My ideal lifestyle is an early to rise day with mediation and personal time, finish work by 3:00pm to spend time with my husband, and time to explore the city.

This vision is authentic, personal, detailed, and value-driven! Values-based visions are so much fun, and they speak to your soul. Visions without values are broad, bland, and leave you without a clear direction. If you don't know where you're going, any road will take you there, right?

Whether your goal is attending the perfect college or traveling the world, having a clear vision that is in alignment with your values allows you to maneuver with clarity, discipline, and authenticity. When you are true to your life, your vision, and what is right for you, you are able to create the life you would want to live.

Xoxo Brittni

Mindfulness

Vision without action is what keeps us in a place of dreaming. Vision needs action; action needs vision. Together, they are what create change and transformation. Without vision and values, a dream is merely a dream.

Understand your values and what is important to you. When you understand what is important to you, you are able to make sure you thoughts and actions are in alignment with those things. This also allows you to be able to watch the company you keep. If your values are different than the majority of the people you know or hang out with, you'll find yourself compromising or doing things that you know you don't really want to do.

Keep the vision for your life true to you and authentic. A vision is backed by tangible goals and an action plan. Breaking down your long-term goals into short-term, measurable goals allows you to hold space for the vision while operating with intentional action. Define what you want, believe in it wholeheartedly, write it down and make it plain, then break it down into steps you can begin taking today. You will reap the fruits of the seeds you sow.

Energy flows in the direction of your focus. These are the results you will manifest whether you give all of your attention to the things you want or do not want. If I were you, I'd send my energy in the direction of what I want to see manifest into my life. Focus positively and enthusiastically on your plan. Stop calling them dreams and get on with your plan. When you use words like, "I'm chasing my dream," it gives the illusion that your goal is eluding you and unable to be attained. This is not true. That vision God has given you, all of those soul urgings and repetitive signs about what you should do, is more than able to be attained. He wouldn't have given it to you if it wasn't. He won't do all of the work for you, though. You are equipped to see this thing through.

Get started. Take action. Move. Hold the vision while you trust the process.

Reflection

Close your eyes and envision your idea of the ideal life.

What does it look like?

_____

_____

_____

_____

_____

_____

Where do you see yourself in 5 years?

_____

_____

_____

_____

_____

10 years?

_____

_____

_____

_____

_____

_____

_____

_____

_____

_____

_____

_____

_____

Now, list your top 10 values that are authentic to you.

1. _____

_____

2. _____

_____

3. _____

_____

4. _____

_____

5. _____

_____

6. _____

_____

7. _____

_____

8. _____

_____

9. _____

_____

10. _____

_____

Now take your values and what speaks to your soul. Write out a values-based overall life vision in present tense. Remember to always act, walk, and talk as if what you are asking for or expecting from your life has already manifested. Use the example from earlier.

_____

_____

_____

_____

_____

_____

_____

_____

_____

Next, take one goal from your vision. State it here:

_____

_____

_____

Make this goal tangible. Making a goal tangible looks like this:

Generic goal: I want to be successful.

Tangible Goal: Success to me is earning $150,000 a year and traveling all over the globe.

Use present tense and make this goal positive.

_____

_____

_____

_____

_____

_____

Create an action plan for this goal. What are you willing to do to see this plan come to fruition? Let the action plan be one you are committed to.

_____

_____

_____

_____

_____

_____

_____

_____

_____

_____

Begin to work on your vision. Repeat this process as many times as you need for your goals.

CHAPTER TEN
Standing Firm in the New

We've gone on this journey together since the beginning of this book. We've assessed our present state of affairs and acknowledged our present way of thinking and being. We've engaged the process to begin change in our lives for the better. We have begun to replace the old with the new. And now, we're here. My greatest hope is that you have opened your minds and hearts to usher in change. I pray you feel free, refreshed, enlightened, and empowered.

I continue to read stories of beautiful, talented, and intelligent young women such as yourself who are going for what they know is theirs. Stories of teen sisters in

California opening their own beauty supply store. Stories of ten-year-old girls selling their lemonade recipes to Whole Foods, stories of young black girls graduating at the top of their classes then going on to work for NASA. I keep hearing of young black girls pioneering engineering programs, publishing books, and showcasing their art in museums – all before the age of fifteen. I keep hearing these stories, and I'm ready to hear yours.

To accomplish these things and more, you must stand firm and unmoved in the new you. You must continue to be a forever-learner, ever-evolving. No one is asking you to be fearless. We are asking you to keep going despite the fear that attempts to keep you stuck and stagnant.

You must embrace your freckles, the texture of your hair, the size of your lips, and the beauty of your skin tone. You must make a decision to embrace the power of your talents, skills, and abilities – whether they come naturally to you or have been learned and studied. You have got to stand firm in the unshakable foundation of who you are. Respect your body and your heart. You have no time for things, boys, or people who do not have your best interest at heart.

Put out into this world that which you wish to receive. Foster your talents, master your crafts, and reject mediocrity. Be the authentic lover, artist, and creator that you were always meant to be. Apply to that prestigious institute and program. Find that cure. Write that code. Establish that non-profit. Clean up that community. Volunteer. Save lives. Speak life. Dance. Pray. Sing. Shout. You are pure perfection manifested. Believe in that.

You can't make others respect the new you or accept your new change, but you can stand in your truth regardless. Black Girl, you can do these and all things. Keep a positive attitude about yourself, others, and the world in general. This will allow you to manifest abundance, peace, love, and harmony. Be the love and change you want to see. This is your chance to awaken to new life. You are a co-creator with God. He has given you the power to speak new life and the authority to bring change to any circumstance. All things are possible with Him.

As I write this, I can literally see all of the faces of the young black girls I know. I can see all of their potential – all the power of their existence. I see my two sisters, my cousins, the daughters of my closest friends, and I see you.

I see each one of you holding this book growing and glowing in light, love, truth, and purpose. I see you excelling, graduating, creating, expanding, and evolving. I see you just being – being still, being talented, being whole, beautiful creatures, and being great. I see the illuminating light of your souls and hearts. I see you bringing this world into a new awareness. I see you achieving and attaining. I see you healing and forgiving. I see you moving on and moving forward. I see you focused, alert, and aware.

There is not one thing you cannot do if you believe in the strength, character, ingenuity, and great power that runs through each strand of your DNA. No matter what your current circumstances may be, you can always change them for the better when you shift your mindset, energy, and focus. You are the next generation of leaders. You are our future. We need you to speak your minds, to care about today's real issues, to make your marks on this world, to care about the environment, and to exude black excellence. We need your originality, innovation, and determination. This world needs your imagination, creativity, insight, and intuition.

You can walk into these classrooms, these courtrooms, these coffee shops, and these auditoriums with your heads held high. You can perform onstage in symphonies, plays, ballets, and the opera. You can start your own businesses, run your own companies, and employ like-minded revolutionaries. It is more than possible for you to start programs for the less fortunate. You can be psychologists, doctors, and professors. There is nothing keeping you from being actresses on top television programs or winning Oscars for your role in major films. You can change the narrative of our people and change the course of what is expected of your peers. You can and you will.

Make us proud young black woman, for you are the essence of perfection.

Xoxo Brittni

Mindfulness

Not everyone understands change. There are people who like things to remain the same. There are people that don't believe in gifts or talents making a way for them. There are people who have never believed in anything – including themselves. Know this: None of that is your problem. None of that is your issue.

This is your life, your day, and your time. You are here, you are ready, and you are equipped to get out here and live. It is time for you to thrive. You are never too young to engage in intentional living. We have created awareness on the journey from the beginning of this book until now. And as you continue to live, learn, and grow, you will become even more aware of who you are and all that life has to offer you. Once you embrace these things, there is no looking back for you. You have every right to thrive. You have every right to make better decisions than those of people around you – this includes family and friends. You every right to live an adventure. You have every right to live life on your terms.

Trust your vision. Trust your heart. Trust your talents and skills. Do not settle or compromise. Align with your true passions and interests. Stand firm and unshaken in this new you – this is where you find fulfillment and joy. This new life change and shift is healthy and much needed. Take charge over the fullness and wholeness of your life.

I answered the calling to dedicate my heart and career to a path that meant something to me – to do what God wanted me to do. You can do the same. Commit yourself to the path that speaks to you. When you embark on the path that is for you, it allows for the joy and abundance you deserve.

Go for it! Follow the signs, take the chances, and risk it all for what you believe in! We need people like you who cause other beautiful minds and to believe and to do. Know your worth and that your existence does make a difference. You should do all of the things in this incredible life that are great, awe-worthy, and life-giving.

The only time we have is now – to be present, creative, and powerful in this moment. Your life and purpose are supported, adored, protected, and guided as you turn your dreams into a reality. Whatever you start now will continue to grow. Your life can and will overflow with all kinds of good.

There is an entire world out there ready for you. And while there is evidence of those who are too afraid to listen to the calls of their hearts, there is also evidence of the ones who have been bold enough to let their hearts lead. Whatever life you would lead if you answered the calling and soul tugging that keeps you up at night, live that.

Cast off old restraints and limited mindsets and be true to you and who have been created to be. Live with great passion, enthusiasm, vigor, and purpose. Focus your energy towards the things you want to attract, toward the life you want to live. Have great knowledge of yourself and establish an authentic relationship with God. The truth of your relationship with your Creator, the truth of your spirit, and the perfection of your soul is the truest beauty.

Don't give yourself the chance to put on any masks. Be you; show up and be real. Bloom from within then put that into everything you do. You have everything you need within yourself. You are a masterpiece now, you are equipped now, and you are capable now. All you have to do is realize, own it, and walk in it. Life is more than your looks, the chaos on the media, what job you'll have, and the empty opinion of others. True life isn't about any of those things. Life is about being – being one with your

Creator, being creative, being greatness, being joy and kindness, being alive in the abundance of loving energy that surrounds you. Your authenticity, God-given talents, and inspired action combined with your open mind, open heart, and the Divine timing of God's plan will fulfill your desired experiences.

There is no lack in you. There is no mistake in you. You are worthy and deserve the best life experience. Love, power, and creation run through your veins. Black Girl, live.

Black Girl, thrive. Black Girl, You Can Do This.

Reflection

How would your new life change you?

_____

_____

_____

_____

_____

_____

How will you feel different?

_____

_____

_____

_____

_____

What is the next step?

_____

_____

_____

_____

_____

_____

What do you know and believe you can do?

_____

_____

_____

_____

_____

Are you ready to live, thrive, and stand firm in the new

you?

EPILOGUE

I initially began writing this book as a love letter to my younger self. I wanted to focus on being for you who I needed someone to be for me when I was your age. But this book became so much more than that. This is a series of love letters, but it also a call to action.

At this age, you are blank canvases of power. Hopefully, now, you have an even better outlook on the life ahead of you. I pray I have equipped you in some way to face life as your best version of you. I hope you accept you and do away with the opinions of others. If you don't, you'll drive yourself crazy allowing the opinions of others to run your life. That is not the life for you. Let all of your feelings about yourself and your life come from yourself. And let these feelings come from a gentle place of truth, originality, and love for all that you are.

You are the generation of change. I have come to cultivate a space of ingenuity and revolution. We need you beautiful, strong, intelligent, and creative young black women to change the course of our people. We need you to help us advance and create a culture of excellence in our communities. We need to see your light, your talents, your skills, and your heart. We need you to walk with confidence, faith, and power. The world needs to see what it really means to be a black girl – unashamed and capable of all greatness. I want you to be able to hit the ground running after reading this book, knowing exactly what it is you want out of this life. A world full of empowered, mentally healthy, loved and loving, emotionally intelligent, and positive-thinking youth is a force to be reckoned with. Defining who you are, now, on your own terms keeps you balanced and focused. Understanding these things now is necessary to be extraordinary.

If you are hurting, be healed. Release and be renewed. Beautiful girl, you can have peace if you simply choose to have it. Your soul is requiring you to heal and make space to transcend past the hurt and confusion of where you may have been – anything unsettling you may have experienced. You must let go of what and who no longer serve you. Gain the lessons from it all, then release all of the hurt. No matter how bleak life may seem, you have the capacity to transform and bring about a new beginning. Forgive yourself, forgive others, take the lessons, and move on.

Understand that your foundation is love. Love is real. Love exists. It is the basis of all creation. Love yourself and others unconditionally. Make love your way of life. We live in such an incredible, powerful, breathing-taking, and beautiful world yet it seems as though all anyone can focus on is lack and everything that can go wrong in the world. Do not allow this to be your reality. There is no shortage of love in this world. Love yourself and every inch of your being – inside and out. You were created in the image of God. It is with His love, wisdom, and Divine creativity that we were created. It is all around us in the sun, the moon, the stars, every tree, plant, animal, and ocean. Focus on that love and let go of the rest. To love wholeheartedly and without condition takes courage. But it is a courage the world needs right now. It is a power – the strongest power we possess. We all have the amount of love we need to love ourselves, everyone, and everything. This love is strong, abundant, prosperous, and ever-lasting.

If you believe you have the ability to change and create a great life of powerful and positive possibilities, now is the time to do so. Experience your life with great love and intention – with great wonder, joy, and awe. Be happy. Happiness comes from within – from being ok with you. You have to be ok with you before you can accept it from anyone else, because others can just as easily take back what they have given. You will sit with yourself for the rest of your life. So make sure you feel your life with self-love and self-care. Be what it is that you want to attract into your life. When you love you first, you'll be able to only participate and accept experiences that are good for you. You will be less inclined to take abuse from others or allow them to take advantage of you. There are so many empty people who never learned the true meaning of love or realized that they are already manifestations of God's love and don't need anyone else to give it to them. I don't want you to be of those people. These types of people will do anything for attention. These types of people become addicted to people, drugs, alcohol, sex, and so many other things – all stemming from a lack of self-worth and a healthy self-love. Be happy.

Protect your body. Take care of it with the foods you eat, the drinks you ingest, and the things you allow yourself to partake in. You only get one body, and it is the home of your soul. Health is about so much more than just what we eat and drink. It is about what we say and do, what we think and feel. Protect and honor your body, soul, and energy on a daily basis. Never settle for negative energies or negative people that may enter your life experience. Do not let pull you into their fear and their doubt, their heart or their pain. Instead, pull them into your light.

God and your angels are always with you. You are never alone. You are protected, loved, and supported. Anything you need, just ask. If you need guidance, clarity, or protection, ask. If you need answers, ask. Quiet your soul and your mind enough to hear what is being said to you and for you. Watch closely to how and where you are being led. Don't worry about a thing – God is always on time with his Divine timing and impeccable wisdom. He knows what you need and will always provide.

Be a forever student, always learning, growing, evolving, and transforming. This life is no race. It is a sacred journey. Everything won't always be easy. That's life – accept it. But you can learn how to roll with the punches and make the most of every situation. If you understood the strength of your God and the blood of the heritage that flows through your veins, you'd never question your ability to handle what comes your way. You have been equipped with everything you need to be everything you have been called to be in this life. Take action! Keep going even when you'd love nothing more than to give up and quit.

There's no value in gossiping, bullying, or maliciously hurting others in any way. That is a lower level way of living, and it is beneath you. When you see injustice in the world, speak up. When you see others hurting, bring them healing. Be the reason others know that they can do and be anything.

Travel this massive world. Try new foods, see new things, learn new languages, and admire new cultures. Meet new people and learn all they have to teach you. Explore the Amazon, climb to the top of the Eiffel Tower, relax on the beaches of Bora Bora, and stay in an igloo in Finland to watch the Northern Lights. Mediate on the sands of Bali, volunteer with elephants in Thailand, try the food in New York, or simply swim in the oceans of Fiji. There is a world outside of your neighborhood, and it is ready for you to come and explore.

Focus on the good in everything and everyone. Even on your worst, most emotional and confusing days, you are still a Queen. Queens thrive. They speak life. They learn and grow. They know how to prosper; they understand they are worthy of health, wealth, and abundance. You are the master of your thoughts, your emotions, and your destiny.

Black Girl, You Can Do This.

ABOUT THE AUTHOR

Brittni Kirkpatrick has always valued authentic living, answering the call on your soul, and using your talents and skills to create the life you desire. Speaking from experience, Brittni made the decisions and mistakes of most teenaged girls. She used these lessons to learn, grow, and empower herself. Her goal now is to guide the next generation of young women to do the same.

Brittni is a Certified Transformational Life Purpose Coach, published author, and mentor. She is based in Atlanta, Georgia where she runs Vibe High and guides clients and students to live to their fullest potential.

46254831R00098

Made in the USA
Columbia, SC
24 December 2018